Night Willow

for Tracie —
listen to the willow 😊

Luisa
04.21.2015

Night Willow

Luisa A. Igloria

ISBN 978-1-927496-05-3

Cover artwork, design and editing by Elizabeth Adams

First Edition
Printed in the U.S.A.
©2014 Luisa A. Igloria

Published by Phoenicia Publishing, Montreal
www.phoeniciapublishing.com

For my daughters

Contents

I

Liminal _____3

This_____5

Compass _____7

Thaw_____9

Blueprint_____11

Augury _____13

Index_____15

To/For_____17

In passing _____19

Sampler_____21

Charmed Life _____23

September 1972 _____24

Rituals_____27

Foster _____29

Poem for Passing Encounters at the Grocery Checkout Aisle_____31

Rotary_____33

Night Willow _____35

Epistle of the Leaves _____39

Redolence _____41

Landscape, with Sunlight and Bits of Clay _____43

Tremolo _____45

Filament _____47

*Despedida de Soltera*_____49

Speaking of __ _____51

II

What Leaf_____55

Letter to Spam _____57

These are the leaves we are hearing now_____59

What We'll Remember _____61

Landscape, with Summer Bonfires _____63

Crossing _____65

Un- _____67

Give me courage, rather, for the leap… _____69

Foolish _____71

Reverence to the Moon _____73

Flush_____75

Precaution_____77

That shore from which we first pushed off, how far away is it now?_____79

Night Watch _____81

Intermission _____83

Lament _____85

Spore_____87

Release _____88

Illusion _____91

Lumen _____93

Midpoint _____95

Dark Body _____97

Santa Milagrita _____99

Paper Cuts _____101

Why appropriation is not necessarily the same as mastery _____102

Conversation that Ends with a Dream of Accounting _____105

Don't_____106

Letter to One Seeking Flight _____109

Working Draft _____111

With Feeling_____113

Hunger _____115

Acknowledgments_____117

About the Author _____119

About Phoenicia Publishing _____121

I

Liminal

"Did I say the day was a sea? I may have meant the day is a diffusion and a scattering of trajectories..." —Seon Joon

Or an inlet. An inlet might be good. Might be a little enclosure, a leading into or away. Marsh, lagoon, bay, sound. Estuary, tide pool, terrace, shelf, strand. As in, to be stranded for a little while with me, myself, and I might learn to work free of pretense, defense— Tonight, if we're going out for dinner, can it be someplace where there isn't a lot of noise? Guinness World Records lists the anechoic test chamber of a lab in Minneapolis as the quietest place in the world. Sitting in the dark in its double walls of insulated steel, concrete, and fiberglass acoustic wedges, you'd hear your heartbeats echoing, your organs paddling in their shallow pools: you become the sound. The longest anyone sat there is three quarters of an hour, before he begged to be released, became disoriented. I believe it. How many times have I woken at dawn from dread spreading through my chest, loud pounding in my ears, the telephone's insistent chime? Scholars, facile with their shiny hoard of new discursive phrases, write of the *liminal.* I lodge there often, where possibility is its most ambiguous flower.

This

This is all you have, this life, this patch of ground marked by wood
and water, a little strand of caterpillar silk caught on low shrubs at
the wood's edge. Everything happens here, or doesn't happen, or
is about to change. Shadows lift at dawn, noon strikes the top of
the stone cherub's head in the middle of the square. Pigeons blend
in among the cobblestones. It's not much, you think: a sleepy
town, the cats in the alley, the same old men playing chess in the
park; the row of tailor shops, the bakers pitching bread into the
fire. The loaves get a little smaller every year, though they remain
as sweet. The lovers with only one place to walk. The seawall. The
pier. The post office at one end of the main street, the market at
the other. Rain drips down every house post and gutter. Flowers
and whitewash on grave markers. You can leave if you want, rent a
room in some city crisscrossed by wires and steel. On every rooftop,
gargoyles opening their mouths to the rain, drinking it all in but
never filling, never filled. Crossing the street, you turn, distracted:
flowering wisteria, japonica, scent spilling urgent messages over
a stone boundary. Nothing leaves, merely decants to color, to
sediment, to underlying pulse.

Compass

It's true then— every word's a compass, pointing at least four
ways; five if you count the rosy bull's-eye that sits in the center:
inscrutable, stubborn or mystical, certainly not letting on. Not
just two, which is what some believe ambivalence to mean. Take
my father's good serge coat, for instance: up close the fine diagonal
weave and ribbing of twill, the relatively affordable sumptuousness
of wool polyester; from a distance, whipcords or pin-stripe
marching down a light grey field. Experienced fingers would know
the difference. He liked to cut a dapper figure, match the colors
in the breast pocket to those of the slip-noose ties. It was a time
when shoes were made of real leather, buffed and shined by spit,
a swipe of polish. The sky in summer had the chalky quality of
canvas. Seersucker and madras, burlap and raw silk— the wind blew
its humid torch equally through every window. The sun wrote its
progress in swirls of turmeric and ink. Heat or no heat, everyone
mostly walked to where they were going. Old history books have
engravings— foreigners in the tropics, top-hatted and walrus-heavy
in their layered suits; their long, spindly legs sheathed in hose,
their women in petticoats and laces. Here, on the first warm day
of spring, I slip into flip-flops and cotton voile. I've snipped the
leather buttons off an old cardigan, saving them for some unknown
occasion in which I might revive their charm.

Thaw

Warmer days, light that fades later and later. Finally we can fling the
windows open. The clasps grate and rasp, like throats gargling salt
water first thing in the morning. Rooms crammed with more than
winter's fat; eaves with bits of leaf and twig, blinds lined with ledgers
of dust. The drawers groan with socks and scarves, the pantry
shelves with unopened cans of beans. I want to scrub all the corners,
scour the tiles in the bathroom with bleach— even the stripes of
grout between each one. I want a pot of yellow strawflowers, a bowl
of blood-red tulips, nothing else but the mellow gleam of wood in
the middle of the room. I read about ascetics and what they chose
to renounce. Sometimes I think I want that. Sometimes I want to
be both the mountains emerging from their heavy robes of ice and
snow, and the streams they feed below, rushing and teeming with
color and new life. Sometimes I want to be the clear unflavored
envelope of agar, other times the small mouthful of sweet *azuki* bean
entombed like a heart in the center.

Blueprint

On this house plan sketched on college ruled paper, I study the
four directions—north and south, east and west, the placement
of doors and stairs. Rooms and hallways must open and close on
auspicious spaces, in order not to create voids. Windows must
open not only to the sun and rain but also to winds of fortune.
What spells do curlicues of dried brome grass press for us to
read against the snow? To ward off evil: water and crystal, wood
and stone, mirrors and discs inlaid with blue glass eyes. In how
many languages could we recite the more than 99 names of God?
Because the eaves of heaven are steep, we need all the help we can
get: celestial guardians to sit at the east, amulets for wealth in the
foyer and on windowsills. A sword to guard the front facing north;
and from the southeastern end of the garden, imagine a merchant
ship steered by the immortals: laden with goods, coming to rest in
the middle of your house.

Augury

The old man wants to know which of his daughters loves him the most.

Like robes of silk? like crackling fat? like sheets of hammered gold with garnet crusts?

Like steel vaults, like a suit of mail, like a dome's marble pillars and carved doors?

Woe to the stammering one who cannot summon her parade of woodpeckers, her retinue of tumbling clowns.

Be careful: bottom-dwellers lurk in the mud, jealous of every bright bubble of original thought.

They'll want to pull her down, cast her out, call her traitor, demoness, ingrate, stupid bitch.

They won't remember it was she who lit the fire in the morning, put the pots to bed at night, filled the glass with water that the indifferent hand reached for and drank.

She fashions a gown out of discarded plastic. She gathers water in a sieve.

Her heart fills and fills with salt— fractals like quivering ribs in magicians' parasols, each more beautiful than the last.

I won't tell her that she'll have her day.

But I watch for signs glimpsed from the high window: how the planets align, how trees cast their shadows along the broken boundary; how the wolves howl as they press closer to their prey.

Index

When the hero of a thousand journeys is born, part of her soul
spirals into a plant that her mother has made to take root in the
soil. A sunflower perhaps. Or a sapling that grows rapidly into a
tree, leaning and breaking into blossom against the wind. Between
every journey is a threshold. Birds bring news of what comes next,
flashing their breasts like pennants rouged with coral or smoke. The
stalk bends and straightens. The flower follows the sun's ascent. The
child climbs trees, runs across the grass, hair flying behind her like
a sheet of night. Milk in the glass still has the sheen of alabaster.
She does not stand in the light of the refrigerator, shifting weight
from one foot to the other, mouth sleepless with frustration or ache
or hunger. In old stories, the elders speak of warriors with heart:
nakem; of growing wiser as *growing in heart*. Perhaps, what they
mean is that capacity not only to survive what gusts in to level us
all— Admit we've traced the fragile vein in the leaf, in the flower;
seen it pulsing at the base of each other's throats.

To/For

Here it is, then: another message to you, sent from this wrought iron table under the dogwood where I sit writing. The birds are masters of solitude or concentration, or ninjas in disguise. They hurtle past, one after the other, intent on one thing at a time. What else would you like to know? I've told you about the secret name I was given in childhood to confuse the gods, so liberal with their gifts of illness and malaise; I've told you about the black sow my grandfather brought from his farm, a gift on my fifth birthday. I'd just been discharged from nearly a month in the hospital— for what, I don't really know and can't remember. They penned the animal in the unfinished bathroom next to the also unfinished kitchen. It kicked at the plywood slats all night. It squealed or bleated, and I thought *That is the sound of what will be sacrificed in the morning.* I didn't see, but I could hear the men sharpening knives and starting a fire by the guava trees. I shut my ears and burrowed into the bedclothes. They were so happy I had been returned, that time had wrought its little miracles. What did I know, and who was I to say that such a feast was not in fact the payment required? I no longer burned with fevers. The purple eruptions on my lips were gone. The animal's shirt of hair would be singed, its insides bled, its sacs of bile and pulsing liver hung up in the trees— dark geodes glinting among the leaves.

In passing

"For the wind blows wherever it pleases… You hear its sound, but you cannot tell where it comes from or where it is going." (John 3:8)

1. The photographs she took reminded her with a start: there was a house below the gate to the army base. There was a *discotheque* in the basement, back in the day when the word was a kind of novelty.

2. One day, they took a walk to the co-op store to buy bread; someone had written on the chalkboard that skinned rabbits were available. On the way back, she picked dry pine needles from the road. She did not ask what was in the dinner stew.

3. When the wind blows sometimes, it brings the insides to the surface— carries the stench of open sewers. You take a breath, you clench, unclench.

4. Our neighbor's daughter thrilled to see the chef toss cleavers, eggs, whole shrimp at the hibachi grill. Metal struck against metal and the heated surfaces of the stove. All show, all show. No real danger in the onion ring volcano, lit to miniature flared explosions.

5. The brass bell swings: small rings of sound under the dogwood.

6. She misses nights sleeping under white mosquito netting, the edges tucked around the mattress; the smell of starched, woven cotton.

7. Dreams and portents: a hand coming out of the dark, searching for another to clasp.

8. Warmer nights now, warmer mornings. Humidity you can smell, rising around the flagstones.

Sampler

* Running Stitch

The hand that spins the yarn has also sanded the frame, has lit the
fire and boiled the morning coffee, has brought the trash to the curb
for pick-up, has started the ignition of the car that sits in rusted
place in the old garage.

* Herringbone

Noon is the hour of making do: smack in the middle of need
and want, those two tips that touch and break, touch and break,
mimicking the hinge in the collarbone.

* Backstitch

The earliest words learned in a new language: body parts, swear
words, words with which to make a promise, words to oil a stone.
Which ones cannot be taken back?

* Chain

You know when someone will change your life: that split second
when an edge makes itself more sharply apparent. For instance, an
upturned collar in the crowd. Then, stepping into the sunlight's
bronze hoops, blinded by something you cannot quite decide—
whether akin to remorse, or pleasure.

Charmed Life

The yard is dusty, Gabriel Garcia Marquez. The chickens have
scratched a path from one side to the other, where it is coolest under
the *sayote* patch and the *bayabas* trees. I cannot sustain a thought as
long as the sentences they write all day in the gravel, back and forth,
forth and back, punctuated only with commas and long dashes. The
honeysuckle bends under the weight of its fragrance. The laundry
hangs on the line, nearly dry. Late last night, coming home on the
road, the car headlights caught swarms of tiny moths in startled
flight. They had such flimsy wings, *kabsat*— they stood out like pale
chiseled ovals, the only movement in the dark. What message were
they bringing? I want to know; or if, high up in the trees, the spirits
watch, waiting to spill their basketful of charms as we pass.

September 1972

This is how it was settled: my father's first cousin, who was some minister or deputy of tourism or other, would help him get a room at the Hilton by the bay. Failing that, his other cousin the congressman had one of his half-dozen apartments in Bel-Air. We could stay in the guest room, which was really his home office. The only caveats: his maid might come in at odd hours to retrieve, from one drawer in the filing cabinet, bottles of black label Johnnie Walker, Courvoisier, bourbon. Also: his Korean mistress might be in town. He borrowed a government car which came with an assigned driver; after all, it was his oath-taking ceremony at the palace.

My mother took special care, ironing his barong between sheets of dressmaking paper. Feeling generous, he told my mother she could bring a friend, but she didn't want to invite any of the women in her various clubs. So I invited Rhonda. We listened to the adults gossip through the six hour trip and drowsed or threw up in paper bags. There was a new and explosive biography about the First Lady, telling of her origins in the south. How she lived in the garage, illegitimate child of the man in whose household her mother served. A few surreptitious copies were making the rounds; the writer had gone into hiding.

Of course it was hot. Even a butterfly pod would shrivel in the shade, split a sleeve open before its time. But still, we fished out our swimsuits and went to bake in the sun by the pool, armed with cheap plastic sunglasses. To hell with heatstroke. We were too young for anything but pineapple juice on the rocks, but the waiters brought them with paper parasols. Rhonda tried to teach me how to affect what she called *an air of worldly ennui*, but I was working through a library copy of *Anna Karenina*. She gave up on me and flopped face-down, on her untanned belly.

The next day, the swearing in itself was a blur; but mostly because someone decided at the last minute that we (women) might not have the protocol clearances. Cousin-congressman and Cousin-deputy went with father. As for us, we returned to the pool and ordered sandwiches and Coke. Mother cooled her bunioned feet in the water and filed her nails. After lunch, father came back and said we had to hustle. *Rumors*, he said. *Best to travel back north before nightfall.* When I think about it now, I realize he was what his contemporaries might have thought a lightweight, not a big stakes player. Too conscientious for his own good, never took a bribe.

That evening, more rumors. Then radio and TV blackouts, and sirens at six and at nine. Not the clarion of the Angelus, but signals for the first of many curfews and the squall ahead. Our sunburned skin peeled for weeks afterward, but nothing of that sort mattered anymore. At home, in the streets where people cast furtive glances at each other, we learned bits of new vocabulary: *martial law, suspension, writ of habeas corpus; rally, molotov cocktail, salvage, subversive, detain.*

Rituals

My hair has thinned, but it's grown longer. I run a sheen of oil across the ends after a bath. That warm haze outside is pollen: floating archipelagos of amber, speckled marcasite, frosted orange. From the closet, I pick a blouse of cotton voile so it might breathe, another skin against my skin. A crow flaps up from the blackcurrant bushes: my first letter of the day! Later, the wind lifts the light higher. A green blush deepens on the hillside. Names of the dead sing through the branches, like needles of pine raining through the air.

Foster

Who's to say what you can believe or not? For every animal of
affection that walks into your ark, its snarling twin pulls at the
chains, trembles the floorboards. You feed them both, you give the
same milk and the same bone wrapped in meat, hunks of bread
to sop up the oil and broth. In the dark, it's hard to tell one from
the other. Their eyes have the same marble sheen, obsidian or clear
grey flecked with green. One will tolerate the length of the journey.
The other will pace and pace, howl at the moon, the rain, the
sun, its shadow. You know it could tear you to pieces if you gave
it more than a chance. But you sing to both, you run your hands
through their sorrowful pelt: this one thing they let you do without
complaint, knowing you too must live in your skin.

Poem for Passing Encounters at the Grocery Checkout Aisle

(after D. Bonta's "Poem for Display at a Police Checkpoint")

The cashier sporting a nose ring and *Kiss Everlasting French Fake
Nails* cracks her gum every few seconds; her high ponytail bobs
as she flips through the three-ring binder and its plastic-covered
product list pages. Finally she asks, *What's that?* pointing to the 4
small purple potatoes I've placed on the counter. After I tell her
and she rings me up, the young man—a high school or college
student working through the summer— bags my purchases. *Paper
or plastic?* he asks, and I say *Paper* to Jihad, for that is what his name
tag says. And I know his name might mean either a holy war or
the struggle of believers in Islam to fulfill their religious duties or
to make believers out of their enemies. But I do not think there
are any *mujahideen* here, no children running through the frozen
food section with homemade bombs strapped under their vests. A
couple of men are buying lottery tickets in the corner, and it's true,
no one ever seems to buy any of the exotic imported fruit marked
at ridiculous prices. The deeply sun-tanned man in the aisle next to
us hefts two six-packs of *Dos Equis* into his cart, and whistles as he
moves to the exit. When he passes I read *Alma y Luz* tattooed with
roses on his right bicep. Behind me, a couple of local firefighters
are waiting their turn with a cart full of pork spareribs, lean ground
beef, and barbeque sauce. One of them picks out a foil-covered
piece of candy from the rack near the chips and magazines. *What?*
he says to his companion; *I love Cadbury Creme Eggs.* And his friend
says *Whatever, man* and laughs.

Rotary

Whirl, I say to the wind, to the red brick wall, to the cobbled street, to nothing and no one in particular. This is the thread I'll tie around my wrist today. Curlicue of an ear, shape of an open palm waiting to cup the notes that blow from a tuba's lip, that croon from a fruit's half-eaten skin. My child stirs *kedgeree* with a fork, fluffing the yellow rice, tapping the sides of the bowl. If only it were as easy to festoon the days with curry, with bits of egg and smoky fish. I'd dangle iridescent earrings to waylay dreams. Across the world, a friend gets up to take another shower. It's a sweltering night in summer: an ice cube has a half-life of fizzle. Meanwhile, here, the ground is glazed with water. The downpour past, the beaches are clean as swept porches. Here come the waves, scrolling their blue-green pages. The carriage rolls back at each interval: *return, return, return.*

Night Willow

(after Beth Adams)

The only ones I knew, those that fringed the man-made lake in my hometown, interspersed with red bottlebrush trees.

I had a sepia print made by an artist friend who passed away— The woodcut showed rowboats on choppy water, the City Hall in the distance; and, distinct at the edges of the frame, the long-fingered leaves of willows.

In their shade, early mornings, an elderly Chinese man came to lead T'ai Chi exercises: single whip, warding off, cloud hands, wild horse spreading mane. Shoes made no sound on the grass.

This is my dream painting: shot through with yellow gleam of lamplights, shadows hunched or hugging their knees like granary gods.

Moss lining the undersides of jagged stones— so even here, it might be possible to say there is still kindness to be found.

Is this what you mean? I've decided to stop knotting up my questions and lobbing them like weapons into the trees.

The sky at night can be the color of ash, can be the color of burnished metal.

If the nest is a purse, then it is so high up in the branches I could not possibly plunder it or probe its depths.

Dear mystery: daily, night after night, I think you're testing me. I won't fight with you anymore.

Branches sough, and shapes of leaves shift in the wind. One by one, daughters will fly away.

Lit, candles burn down into bowls of liquid wax, even as their smoky fragrance lingers.

Tell me in your own time what you want to say.

Landscape, with Things Falling from the Sky

It ticks, the iris underneath: the heavy-lidded eye in its leathered
sac blinks open, mercurial, at the slightest touch. So falls the sky in
fable: as a leaf, as a flutter of feathers, as an acorn pinging across a
table of rock. Fear is the room where it all echoes. Or love. A galaxy
is only a dark umbrella someone opens so rain can streak the grass.
When all the water's gone, the ribs shine dull silver. In the spaces far
between are stars.

Epistle of the Leaves

"Take courage, Holy Parents of Pharcitae, udes adonitas —
no one is immortal."
— *Inscription in the Cave of the Coffins, Beit She'arim*

Bindwood, lovestone, grief's greenest eraser: see how the slightest wind
ruffles the ivy. See how they flourish on walls, erupt in every breach,
more unruly than graffiti. So many signatures, cascading. In the
trees, a bird sings one, sad note and snaps a brown moth out of
the air. Who authors the scope of what can be seen or told? I read
how Newton took a bodkin and put it *betwixt the eye and the bone*
as neare to the backside of his eye as he could. Imagine the circles of
color that pulsed beneath his lids on the verge of light: *white darke,*
blewish darke. The eye was not hurt, he wrote. Though at the fall
of feathers, a sifting of soft dust from the sill or the eaves, the hand
instinctively flies up to cover the face— So the green tendrils pin
their fragile geometry against the gate, admitting what the soul has
done in its defense.

Redolence

Delicacy: faintest tinge of flavor, the way I know what words can make you blush. Mostly for their smell, last summer I planted verbena between the mint and roses. The weeds look almost tipped with silver and the moon is coppered thin. I sit in the window bay waiting for the heat to dwindle, to sweeten in the clover. Do you know why the green herbs stitch their tiny shadows on the sill? After the storm last night, all the lights went out, down the length of the street. Warm amber, warm musk, sweet hook: your scent in the dark.

Landscape, with Sunlight and Bits of Clay

Because I admired a glazed plate veined with obsidian and blue-green, my friend took me to visit a potter in his studio. He worked the local clay, prodded the wet mass on the wheel into a wide-lipped vessel from which to pour the milk or wine, mugs from which to drink, dishes to hold warm slabs of meat or beautiful smoked fish as if they merely leaped from the cold arms of the river entire, as if their iridescent, speckled bodies did not thrash when the air left their lungs... I read of how long the Buddha sat in the canopy as leaves of the bodhi tree fell on his plain robes, fell in the dust at his feet, or swirled away in runnels of rain— until the torch of desire burned clean and the pulse in the wrist marked time like the faintest fragrance in the wind. I don't know that I have learned yet what the green fists of bracken in the grass have learned, how to open their complex fingers to the sting of rain as if to say *Let it come*— Sunlight gilds every surface today but also knifes through every anguish; and I don't know who or what I address as I lift my face and say *Not yet.*

Tremolo

Dear invisible hand scribing the surface of this vinyl platter, you
usher in a new soundtrack: buzz of a black-throated warbler,
catbird's brassy solo. All cool and nonchalant— but underneath: the
faltering notes of what we want so much to say but can't. Fluttering
skin, stroked by feathers. If I begged you to stay, if I begged you to
take me away? What then? But I don't. In the evenings, the crickets
repeat their two-note arias. Under the trees, fireflies send stuttering
messages across the dark.

Filament

Anything voiced against the wall of a whispering gallery will be audible to a listener standing diagonally on the other side. Look for a place where two pathways intersect, where a vaulted roof forms a shallow dome. In a story I once read, a man spoke just under his breath to a woman across the room. His secret kindled like a flame as though he were by her side, or inside. The sides of the cupola are blue with shadow, but the pillars have the warm tint of citrus. Marble is veined, and not always cold. You'd think a low murmur might carry faster through uninhabited rooms; but it finds its way, even in a thicker medium. Just fling a window open. Let the heavy curtains learn to babble in the wind. Listen to the low-key chattering match of nuthatches a hundred yards apart. Outside, flakes fall through the air—just enough to leave the barest fur on the ground, like a leaf's glaucous bloom.

Despedida de Soltera

Three of my four music teachers were nuns. And the neighborhood referred to my very first piano teacher as the spinster— she wore dark clothing, sensible shoes, *agua de colonia flor de naranja*. She lived alone, with only part-time help; she never told anyone where she went in summer: *Soltera*. But I've always preferred this nod to solitude, to single-tude; the way impudent "l" pushes away from gossipy "o" and fakely coy "e" to bump up against "t" as if to say— *So what?* Years later, I'm still amazed at how much they knew: the libraries of trills and crescendos hidden underneath wimples and lace shawls; the ways they coaxed feeling from generations of wooden pupils surreptitiously kicking their legs into the piano's soundboard. Listen to the advance of notes in this passage, they'd say: surf shirring the sand, or horses' hooves soon coming around the bend. And then the clearing drenched in the scent of violets, which moves you inexplicably to tears. From my bedroom window, the chair-backs in the garden are scrolled like treble clefs. It's still mostly dark when the first faint pink spot appears in the clouds. I lie within that brief interval of solitude just before the day begins, slow and red. A raven croaks.

Speaking of __

Let us lower our voices, said the woman next to me at the bus station; *but I know what you are speaking of.* Hammock strings have a way of recoiling. Is that when we can no longer lie in it? Then we might go indoors to make the meal, call the children in, unfold the blankets against the night's chill. Even so there will always be that one place you'll want to keep setting at the table, the room that will become a shrine. You'll never catalogue the growing things on that stretch of roadway, how many pieces of glass were rendered from the *kuatro kantos* bottle; what restraints might multiply in the hands of another. I am sorry too. Resemblance does not often matter. Money? Sex? It could have been a simple thing, the chrome of a radio dial sticking out of a jacket pocket. I listened this morning to stories of refugees trying to cross the desert; a woman's sobs woke me from sleep. From over the ridge, a patrolman's amplified voice, his words unintelligible. There are places in the world where a blue jay does his best impression of a red-tailed hawk, and then departs. Something like wings scissors in the sunlight. *Oh my poor poor sweetheart,* moaned the woman in the desert, over and over again; *I could not even bury him.*

II

What Leaf

What leaf is small and black and falls more slowly than a feather?
What ink washes deeper blue then sable as it nears the shore?
What crystal spangles every lidded eye on trees and bushes?
What letter writes itself over and over in the wind?
A fire dances up in the trash burner, the brightest thing.

Letter to Spam

(a found poem)

Can you keep a secret? They will never know. In my e-mailbox at
work this morning, this message: When wearing one of *Practically
Genuine's* clones, you won't have to worry about being caught. How?
We manufacture all our products (from the inside/out). Using the
same metals, markings, materials as the originals ensures the perfect
clone. In 1936 the pantywaist was a type of child's garment with
short pants that buttoned to the waist of the shirt. In Old English,
a stole is a long robe, a scarf-like garment. Clergymen wore it.
Frankly, I much prefer the sixteenth century use of doublet (root,
Fr. *duble*) as "one of two things that are alike." Keep this quiet and
your friends, family, co-workers, and loved ones will never know
the difference. Six inches of fresh powder. A pair of squirrels will
wrestle in it, then go up the big maple, couple on the trunk, retreat
to separate limbs. All those little gropings in the shadows. Do you
need a translator? Think of it. History is full of copies, some of them
cutting themselves out of the landscape right now.

These are the leaves we are hearing now

The kitchen boy comes out of the restaurant door, swinging a bag
of trash. On the way to the dumpster he pauses under the crepe
myrtles in full and premature flower, under the magnolias and
their profusion of heavy blooms. It's nearly midnight but the heat
is thick as a double velvet drape in an old-time movie theatre, and
the sounds of rasping in the trees are like instruments being tuned
in the orchestra pit. The cooks have gone home, and the sushi chef.
Only the waitresses are still inside. The security guard with the name
of a crone comes out of his car and walks around the parking lot,
peers into the lit windows of the sports store. The Pho restaurant's
been closed since nine; the sign in neon-colored chalk advertising
their new bubble tea has muted to one shade: that of a rusty hinge.
Hidden from view, a hundred forewings translating texture; tymbals
rasping along the insect's abdomen, to make the sound of the leaves
we are hearing now.

What We'll Remember

We'll remember this as the summer when hail rained down as large
as peaches, when whips of lightning tore through the humid air.
We'll remember this as the summer when we woke and looked up
to see a sky filled with clouds in the shape of women's pendulous
breasts; when every day as we walked from one end of the field to
the other, it seemed the cicadas' agitated chirping might rival the
noise of oncoming trains. And we'll remember this as the summer of
startling sightings: wild birds far from home, a man-of-war sailing
into the harbor, cannons firing in salute; and a body washed up on
the river's edge. A cerulean warbler sang incessantly in the yard, and
doctor's reports recommended the cutting away of some parts. We'll
remember this as the summer of swiftest change: how we walked,
mornings and evenings, past fences overgrown with wisteria— their
opulent scent already balanced on the rim of decay.

Landscape, with Summer Bonfires

In the foyer, rippled leaves like giant seaweeds droop. Who
remembers to water the plants when everyone is gone? The
air-conditioning sends chilled drafts down, but the heat of high
summer is yet to come. Overhead, the skylight's a square of
marbled white, like some trapdoor in the basement of the gods.
The first fire-stealer broke off a branch of glowing coal, embers
hidden in a fennel stalk, falling headlong with it back into the
world. *Take that,* he spat to the vengeful ones. At the edge of the
park, eagles circle overhead and return to the same tree. If you
raise your binoculars, you can see them bring back things in their
beaks, shred pieces of meat for their hungry young. And the liver,
oh the liver: peck it out to nearly nothing and still it grows back.
See if you can stop the history— Trains and ironworks rushing
forward, sparks' hot striving from struck metal. Hibachis firing
up, backyards soaked in the smoke of summer barbecues and shish
kebabs, scritch of a match on the sole of a shoe; bonfires staining
the woods defiant red, even as the sun goes down.

Crossing

What could I say when you asked what made me startle in the
night, what made me throw off the makeshift quilts you pieced
together of touch, so I could sleep? In the old days, dreams were
more than just dreams: they were portents, omens, doorways
creaking open into the unknown-becoming-known. In the stories
there are always doors. There is always someone saying *Choose*, and
there is always someone either walking into the maw of a hungry
beast ready to flay her alive, or into a garden hung with scent, fruit
bending, glamorous as comets festooned to branches. Who is to
say which one brings sudden death, which one turns on a flood of
unending light or sets the stars careening across the sky? A breeze
unleashes a shower of petals and they fall upon the ground. And
even the leaves— one side yellow, one side green— are hinges: tell
me what their veined surfaces say before the heart swings open and
collects them for the afterward.

Un-

The stamp on the creased letter read: *No forwarding address.*

Three cypress trees whose roots grew networks in cracked sewer pipes (the landlady sent two men to chop them up).

Two maple keys dangling in an old spider web: remnants of a winged creature's wings.

Assorted metalware (25,000 light bulbs, 6,000 vinyl records, 2 gold rings) in an 80-year-old Serbian stuntman's stomach. And the bike pedal that did him in.

The world's largest pig hairball and two deformed calves, sitting in glass cases in an abbey.

Last year we read of cheese and ice cream being made from human milk; the other day: an article on cat owners knitting cardigans from spun, shed fur.

That faint smell of wet dog? Probably mildew from the water reservoir in the steam iron you use to take wrinkles out of traveling robes.

Truthfully, I'd rather wash than iron: soap and water, dirt wrung through the cord. The iron's false promise: uncreasing some small part of life. Singed polyester therefore a kind of revenge.

Give me courage, rather, for the leap...

Not a fugitive, not a mole that has burrowed away from the light,
into the soil— no wraith in a cave, I've chosen to live above ground.
What are my truths? Don't look for platitudes hanging cheap as
baubles on any shrub. I've had to strike out farther, deeper; carve
paths not favorable to the flesh of my hands. What was it for? Only
to live a life under the aegis of other terms. No wealth to report,
only weary. Neither bluster nor bravura: I still flinch like never
before. Perhaps you would have done differently? perhaps you
would have obeyed? perhaps you would have thought it unnecessary
to keep in sight that porthole of changing light? Over and over, I've
tried to outline— so many mouths that murmur in the dark, so
many things to disclose. The real calculus isn't even configured; who
is it you were looking for, again?

Foolish

"In a painted sea, what to write? A letter taking tomorrow back?"
—D. Bonta

When the tide was low, I walked and loved the water and the sugary sand. When it was high, I stayed my careful distance and fingered threads, turned pages, steeped tea, listened to the murmur of voices in public rooms. They came and went, as if there were no tomorrow. I loved the varied colors of their customs, their buttonholes and hatbands, the air suffused with smells of tobacco leaf or oranges or lavender; I loved their dark heels of stacked wood, their calves wrapped in supple leather. Wind sped through the trees, which shed their leaves then budded as the season turned. Once, flying in as evening broke and the cities below filled out their grids with light, I watched as a couple kissed and kissed in their airplane seats. They sank into each other as if the air was tasteless, as if the sky was lackluster, as if their need for delirium was the color of the sun as it seized then disappeared at the rim of the sea. I wish you were foolish with me like that, I wish you'd come to me as if I were the last cool drink of water forever and forever in the world.

Reverence to the Moon

The birds started singing before five. Morning shuddered into light, cool air.
What animal rolled up its shirtsleeves and pilfered the lock of the cage, its hair
matted as night, its breath the color of knives? Smoke and bombs in the street,

screams, broken glass. The saint, in her lifetime, hardly wore shoes on her feet.
She walked the streets to touch the sick and dying, the young and old; the cat
licking its wounds in the alley, mewing for a bowl of milk— Anyone who forgot

how the moon could spill its honey to overshadow the lamps by the bay;
and still there will be more. Wreckage and debris, charred ashes that grey
each stone on the ground. In a stampede, dust the color of gold.

O love, o neighbor, o stranger huddled in fear and waiting for parole:
how much more we belong to each other. How we wait to be consoled.

*

Flush

Love is the opening of the heart, the welcoming of your beloved.
Birdling, tiny thing that bumps head-on, unwittingly, into the
glass— you are not yet the announcing angel. Like you I've been
distracted by the flicker on surfaces, yellow-green, light-dusted,
feathery as eyelashes. What do you see as you stop to take a breath,
as you teeter, then center, weight full on the ledge? Indentations
in the stucco: imperfect, unlevel— clumsy as a new lover's caress,
yet punctuated with ardor. I lie beneath the sill, hair in disarray,
attempting repose. It is either the moment before or the moment
after. When you find your bearings and flit away, your shadow
mimics the pulse fluttering at my throat: momentary touch, what
visited there last.

Precaution

It's that paper-thin hour just after rain, and the windows are open,
and fragments of sky are visible behind a haze of leaves. One by one
the lights come on in houses down the way. The odors of supper
fill the air: charred meat, boiled potatoes, onions. The smell of
wilted greens does not carry clean, unlike the tang of mint from
the garden, the neighbor's jasmine. A voice on the radio talks of
this time last year, the soldiers raiding the fugitive's safe house, the
helicopter letting them down in the cabbage patch. The burial at sea
with no witnesses. And now the neighbor is working on his back
gate, taking advantage of the good hour or so of remaining light.
Lately, he's taken to smoking Cuban cigars; the sweet, leaf-smoky
note adds itself to what's gathered: an odd bouquet. He's put in a
small solar panel attached to a motion-sensor light. The frame of
white plastic tilts up among the ivy. I watch as he tests it and it
flickers on, a warning flare of yellow.

That shore from which we first pushed off, how far away is it now?

In the morning, by the kitchen door, paper-thin strawflowers hold out their yellow bowls. The brass bell I bought from a temple gift shop swings under a branch of dogwood: a little more weight every day, as shoots erupt and buds crack open. Even verdigrised, you'd think the light is mild, is mellow, brings nothing but the gooey oil of blessings. Who's to say it isn't so? And yet, and yet. Even when the wind keens like the tool of a glass-cutter bent on dividing surfaces into a liturgy of smaller parts, a screen assembles. Don't add my name yet to the names of the dead on the wall. Don't carve their letters edged in gilt on a crypt. Just today, I thought of how, in place of a fence to put up around a yard of my own, I'd plant jasmine— so when its asterisks of scent opened on warm nights, no one could tell where their beauty or their yearning for the other side began.

Night Watch

And if I say *heat, expected rain, lassitude*— the hollows of my bones
begin to mimic the throats of brittle plants. I was seized by thirst,
reading a catalogue of inks: morning glory, transparent blue as
raindrops on its cheek; moonlight, brazen crimson of azaleas. Purple
berries, named after the lady-in-waiting who wrote the first novel.
The names of women were not even recorded in her time. I think
of her, restless on her sleeping mattress, mining the indigo shade of
night after night for illumination. Green sentinels of bamboo; ochre
fields, stalks bursting with grain— each pointed like a nib.

Intermission

It's late. It isn't yesterday anymore. The hour has moved beyond
that part of the sundial. Up in the woods, soon the witch hazel
will leaf a low green flame. Yesterday we picked our way through
hellebore, through foxglove, through belladonna. Above, the
heads of snowball viburnum drooped low like lanterns. I turned
a question I cannot voice over and over in my head. No one will
hear its soft bumping in the corners, no one but me see the flare of
orange tracks in the velvet dark. If I said it aloud, all this softness
would fade in an instant. The lambs' ears would shrink and recoil,
the creeping flox and the tiny fingers of salt cedar form crystals like
ice. See the roses massed on the trellis, the rows of spiked thorns on
guard at their feet.

Lament

What I would give to be a vein on the side of the red maple whose
leaves tremble in the wind— I want to be plucked like that again,
tuned to singing. The bees stumble into the storm door and later,
there are clumps of yellow, tracks the color of fenugreek or pine
bombs or birch. Little pools by the road film over with pollen,
daubed thick as paint. The light can hardly strike where all this
matter congeals. I cannot ignore it. I cannot turn away. I want to
scour every pot I own until each grainy bottom reflects a face which
used to match the corona of blue flame heat for heat, glare for glare.
Every now and then I crave the iron taste of swamp spinach, the
thin scraps that tether marrow to the inside of bone. Something
true, unapologetic; something that doesn't merely settle into the
background, fade into the atmosphere, trick you into thinking this
is all there can be, and nothing more.

Spore

At lunch in the Chinese restaurant: couples with salt-and-pepper
hair (the women in modest pumps and tweedy jackets and the men
just loosening their ties), babies in high chairs, teens in tunic tops
not even teetering in their absurd stiletto heels. A veil of sesame oil
in the air, the clatter of dim sum carts. The child says— *I wonder
what you'll look like when you're older?* On the way here, we passed
the Woodlawn Cemetery and I couldn't remember if that was
where the writer who was a diplomat in his other life was buried.
Many years ago I spoke with him a few times over a crackly phone
connection; me in graduate school, acorns pinging from the trees
as autumn in the Midwest made the branches ready for a long
sheathing in ice. He must have been in that nursing home where
he died. I did not know then about the daughters they said had
left him there then disappeared, the nurses unable to trace them to
any forwarding address. He told me he walked to the local library
as often as he could, a yellow legal pad under his arm. In the latter
part of his life, he scoured the shelves for poems, copied them out
by hand. He complained he could not find anything by René Char.
I think I might have sent him a book, translated poems found in
one of the used bookstores up on Clark. *le Poème pulvérisé?* I can't
remember now. I knew about his hasty exit from Cambodia just
before the fall, he and his wife with one suitcase each. The former
dictator's government never made up for his losses, those years
of faithful service. I must repeat, I never really met him. He was
a voice on the phone, a voice I imagined when I read his stories.
Often I wonder if he ever thought this would be a place as good as
any, in which to die.

- in memoriam, Manuel A. Viray

Release

*"My knuckles are raw in the wash-water, my hips ache
with a thousand unbirthed hopes." —Seon Joon*

You dream that your father, long dead, walks out of the bathroom.

He's clad in his terry-cloth robe the color of light ochre, the color
of pollen shaken from the stamen of a common flower whose name
you have forgotten.

It's barely morning, the sky just shading into a faint silvery blue.
Like periwinkles washed by rain, the fragile garment of their petals
thin as breath.

Why are you here, you want to ask, *what is the meaning of your visit?*
But he has gone to sit by the window in his favorite chair; he closes
his eyes, begins fingering his rosary. You do not think it is proper to
disturb. You let him be.

In the middle of a dream like this you know you're watching your
heart move through a landscape mostly hidden from view.

You know you've been the snail, rolling the evidence of everywhere
you've been into a narrow ribbon. Would you call this economy, or
efficiency? So much, crammed into such a miserably small space.

Everything fit into this spiral shell of echoes, plus some. You heard
the water in the dishwasher. Tremulous sounds coming over the
trees. Cars slowing down on the cobblestones, the high-pitched
whistle of a train approaching. Two women quarreling, always
quarreling, in the same house. The neighbor taking his dog in from
a walk.

It's time to go, children; pack up your work, your notebooks, your
things. There are thumbprints on the edge of the wooden desk. The
drawer is full of pencil shavings. Soon the trees will thicken with
leaves or birds.

You want to empty the blue plastic buckets standing under the rain spout. You want to feel their round, palpable heft as you tip them over the stones and the cool water floods the empty garden plots.

You want to feel the weights released from each hand, the pulley-ropes gone slack. A line almost of sweetness, the shock rippling from your wrists to your hips.

Illusion

Even the eye could forget its tears, the mouth its fondest
lamentations. Face pressed, attentive, to the glass. The world's
a wheel, a shadow box, a zoetrope with slits through which we
glimpse a strip of paper where horses and birds are drawn. The
wind spins it around, or waves of air rising warm from the lamp
on which it rests: cunningly, limbs leap from frame to frame, crest
obstacles, fluoresce. But there's no other word for this wobbly
apparatus of our discontent.

Lumen

Showers of white dust. Blossoms shredding soft as paper from
overhead, lighter than suffering. Let them fall where they will. Let
the bent head accept this windfall. Let the light shift and refract
through the makeshift scope.

Midpoint

The hour will come, oblivious to your noticing, when you'll look
back and see that the shore is truly far away and the boat you're
in, bobbing miles from any clear destination. From that distance
it will be hard to tell what the sunlight strikes hard and fractures:
the chrome edge of a pair of sunglasses, the unibrow of the man
wearing it, the neon stripes of the beach umbrellas that now look
ridiculously small and crowded around the rim of a dirty yellow
margarita glass. And you will ask, stranded in the middle of it all,
whether you really still need sunblock or if the little stencils of color
floating before your eyes are a sign— everything that once pinned
you to the business of diminishing returns has called it quits. Now
only this expanse, its lesson unrolling like a sutra: *unfurnished,
unambiguous, pithy, comprehensive; continuous, without flaw.*

Dark Body

Dark-promised, soot-colored, life-size statue of the *Nuestro Padre Nazareno*— Clear sky, bright sun that stripes his rickety carriage, borne on the shoulders of hundreds of men. Carpenter, boat-builder, cop and cobbler; plumber, electrician out of work, not yet sober *tuba*-drinker; husband, overseas worker, skirt-chaser, wife-beater. They've all come to touch this visage of coal, this visage of charred ship lumber. Fire translates into scars on the body's timber. Any piece of clothing will do to daub its flesh-like surfaces: torn t-shirt, scrap of cotton, burlap sack, polyester, old gym towel. They pull on ropes, conveying this likeness cloaked in saffron and red velvet. In the choked streets, see how urgent the desire to touch, be touched, be filled with fleeting grace. Some have fainted. Some have lost a finger, crushed a rib, a clavicle. For miracle, what does it matter that one might be trampled?

Santa Milagrita

Here's a heart cut out like a cookie made of tin, ringed and pierced
with holes: through it, the light shines— like ornament, like a
bauble wrapped in foil. Its cold fluted layers gleam and pleat, like
the halo of a small town saint who's made good and come back to a
hero's welcome: so many tokens at her feet, so many supplicants in
parade. The traffic never stops at her wayside shrine: *bring me back
my lover, my daughter, my mother,* that life of promised ease. Here, in
exchange, all these glittering anatomies: fingers, arms, legs; an eye,
an ear— parts we would lop off gladly; if only, if only.

Paper Cuts

Let's fold and crease the paper, once here and once over. Remember cutting half the outline of a paper doll then watching a chain of them shake loose in the air? Identical in bobbed hair and pleated skirts, hand in hand in hand, soon nubile-breasted. On the edge of the lake, a dark-haired woman walks barefoot, skimming stones and feeding bread to the swan draped around her shoulders. Winged silhouettes are always harder to do, so this time let's try sheets of ice shaved into snowflakes. Cut out the shapes of prisms through which the light can fan, clear and cold, feathered lace against the skeletal branches. Hold them up against window glass: such flimsy tokens that we offer at the turnstile, as we pass.

Why appropriation is not necessarily the same as mastery

The child wants to know the names of all the herbs and spices on the shelf: those roots floating in a jar like a stunted man treading water, those dried leaves twisted carelessly with twine and left in the kitchen drawer.

Sounds made in a different tongue are often so enchanting— at the start, they are like rain falling, plinking over looped chains in the garden.

Remember that things have names. It is important to know that one thing will not always substitute for another. The beautiful berry leaves a dark stain on the tongue, a body lifeless in its bed.

Remember that a syllable can be slighter than an eyelash. The way it flicks up or down can mean a question, or your chin.

The violinist recounts a fairy tale of a boy kept years with others like him in captivity. They buff the witch's floors to the sheen of glass, gather the fine amber dust in the air to bake into bread, the dewdrops in the hearts of roses to feed her unslakeable thirst.

Later, trying to remember, the one bewitched says phrases over and over. But there is no one there to catch his mistakes, to help him put the pieces back together.

And you, you've been such a good student of that epistemology, of thinking-into-being: don't you know that spells are made of words?

Remember too: not all saying is true.

I have heard another story: how the Pont de l'Archevêché groans with the weight of hundreds of padlocks, etched with promises made to eternity. What happens when the language of the promise is wrong, when the word for "expensive" is used instead of "love?"

Do you glimpse my original shape beneath this overlay of form? The rain falls and falls over the village. The tailor sews in his shop, the fiddler plays a tune by the fire.

Arrival is recognition, which brings a catch in the throat. We weep when words break through a surface. We weep when we have seen ourselves.

Conversation that Ends with a Dream of Accounting

All these years. How many years? Ten? Eleven? That's great. No, I
don't have a portfolio. How great that you could spend so much
time on vacation. White sands. I was there just once: centuries
ago. No, I've never been to that Marina. I saw your pictures at the
infinity pool. That's cool. It's hard to take time off; it catches up to
you. I've often wondered, why are all the people in your photos, in
restaurants all the time? And everyone with a cell phone. The waiter
is a vegetable vendor? He's putting himself through school? I'm
tempted to ask if he will stock my mother's pantry every Monday.
At her age, she prefers fruit and green leafies. She texts me every
few weeks to say her cupboard's getting bare: *Send money.* Where's
that tree with bills clipped to the leaves, which passersby hardly
notice? I'm gripped by spasms that keep me from falling asleep at
night. And when I do, I dream of accountants pursuing me with an
abacus in each hand. They're dressed in grim or grey, but the beads
click like hungry teeth in Day-Glo colors. You know I've never been
good at numbers. I used to know but have forgotten how to reckon
by them— something about ones, tens, hundreds, thousands:
expenditures on one hand, omissions on the other.

Don't

We don't have a language brave enough to address these things:
hot breath inches away from the face, the names that shift the
indeterminate pestilence of hate through streets and school halls,
the taunts that masquerade as jokes, the protocol in place for rolling
with, moving on, getting over it—

We don't have a language to talk about the color of those parts
underneath the clothes, underneath the skin; the parts themselves,
the sound those parts make as they congeal in a mouth where the
hurt of teeth is fresh memory from a fist—

We don't have the words to make sense of any contradiction of
parts— black hair, green pupils, slanted eyes— resulting in a chase
from the bar and out through darkened streets, the baseball bat
swinging and swinging to make repeated contact with *alien* skin—

We don't have a language for the silence that resounds afterward
where there should be response, the silence a pall in those marbled
rooms where justice has not been served; the silence hovering like
a mouth above every fresh-made grave, the weird silence in the
streets though there are people on the sidewalks when a band of
motorcycle riders rushes a van to beat its occupants, just because—

And we don't have a language for that great, mad noise which
should burgeon high over the walls like that noise made by Godzilla
or by Godzilla's mother, whose brain and limbs I'm sure were also
fried when the bombs fell over the South Pacific— She may not
be in the movie but I tell you she exists somewhere, bellowing the
primitive syllable of her pain, our pain, for the lesion delivered to
one is delivered to all—

And we don't have the adequate language for the different ways
we're daily taken hostage, dangled by the feet over the abyss as
penny puppet show, as entertainment for the black-tie crowd—

Which is why it is so hard to stumble home and tell ourselves, tell our children, *Love is all we need,* for we cannot part our pain from all the great love bombed out of our hearts—

And we don't have enough reserves of language for that either, we don't know where and how to start to tell each other what we must, which is *Enough, enough, enough, enough, enough*—

Letter to One Seeking Flight

The soul's wilderness is ringed by pine and rugged cliffs above which birds with wings stronger than mine circle and circle the primed canvas sky. They give me their surplus of feathers— dress remnants of silky black, ink grey, satiny pearl. I find them strewn carelessly in the discount racks and rush to gather them up. I study them closely to make adjustments— ah what I wouldn't give right now for even a jar of Gorilla Glue or a hot glue gun, in lieu of a crossbar and wires, battens, a keel. Something that noses into the wind and lofts quick with the changeable currents, to take me away from here. It's cold at sunrise: that time of day when the honey and the wax need most prodding (I've come across tiny striped bodies, asleep in their padded cells). My arthritic hands need warming too. They hurt intermittently, as though these fingers were carving labyrinths from stone. It's always more difficult at night, or in the long winter months when the light slants, elusive, in the cave. And yes, that crazed bull likes to sit in the mother of all mazes, making frightful noises: uncombed, unwashed, unkempt. But, surprise— it unravels too. All it takes is one skinny thread, one end of yarn poking up from the corner of your brightest red sweater. It works something like a ripcord. Pull on it. Or wear it and see what happens.

Working Draft

So you could fall asleep, I whispered stories in your ear. I made
them up, each one a new letter flying in the window from another
world. I don't remember any endings, only how they began: slight
figures moving (I hoped, bravely) against a landscape. Even then,
the first rule of narrative: something has to happen, then something
has to give. The bowl that was empty filled and filled. I gave what
I could, for what good was it, locked away in a safe? But the street
overflowed with briars. The sea came up the walk. Wings beat the
air, taking away the one thing that was loved most. *That is how
it goes, that is how it goes*. And then when I am gone one day you
might open a drawer and find a pearl in the shape of a tear.

With Feeling

So what if the beautiful ones always sit in the first row, where the
lights strike their hair and jewels the brightest? So what if their
fathers have paid for the places they occupy, with little regard
for how much it costs others? They post selfies with captions like
"Thing is, I don't give a shit." The potted trees in the atrium are
equally beautiful for having no memory of origins. They breathe
in the temperature-controlled air but do not bend their branches.
A little boy pees in the terra cotta basin, unable to keep it in any
longer. Outside, a storm begins its orchestral arrangements: tympani
and brass; winds. But night's darkest tuxedo is the mother of all
corporations. I want to tell the guard who ushers out the errant
boy and his crestfallen parent, *You are mistaken.* It is holy to feel
the visceral coursing through you, unstoppable like wind or water.
If you ever opened your mouth to the rain, perhaps you might
understand how a string stretched as if near breaking gives off that
depth of sound. Think of it like stars rushing through the roof.
Think of the solitude of the lonely, the destitute, the ailing. Then try
to play it again: the kind of music that trembles the skin, escapes the
strictures of syntax.

Hunger

Breakfast of weak morning light, trickle of coffee. Steam from heat vents along the street. Tendrils of hunger. Gently I push them down, move them to the back. I say *Later, later.* And it's later, and I'm still saying *Later,* though the sun is high and the clouds now move across the sky, puffs of mousse on a Magritte platter. One of them looks like a young hare: white on white, hunched around its hunger. Another's corded like the shell on which the goddess floated, like foam on the skin of water. Meanwhile my insides are gnawing on the leaf of impatience. Its veins are green and have no dressing; and butter does not always make everything better. What do I want, what do I need? *Later,* I tell myself, *later.* There's plenty of work, the hours full of obligation. But I know I am not virtuous: I am always my hunger.

ACKNOWLEDGMENTS

Earlier versions of some of these poems appeared in
Via Negativa (www.vianegativa.us) between November 2010
and September 2013 as part of my poem-a-day project.

Special thanks / Mil gracias / Maraming salamat to
Dave Bonta (*Via Negativa* and *Morning Porch*),
Elizabeth Adams and Phoenicia Publishing.

About the Author

Luisa A. Igloria is the author of *Ode to the Heart Smaller than a Pencil Eraser* (selected by Mark Doty for the 2014 May Swenson Poetry Prize; Utah State University Press); *The Saints of Streets* (University of Santo Tomas Publishing House, 2013); *Juan Luna's Revolver* (University of Notre Dame Press, 2009 Ernest Sandeen Prize); *Trill & Mordent* (WordTech Editions, 2005); and eight other books. She holds degrees from the University of the Philippines, Ateneo de Manila University and the University of Illinois at Chicago, where she was a Fulbright Fellow from 1992-1995. She teaches on the faculty of Old Dominion University and currently directs the M.F.A. creative writing program. Since November 20, 2010, she has written (at least) a poem a day; the poems are archived at Dave Bonta's *Via Negativa* site.

The author's website is at www.luisaigloria.com, and her poem-a-day project can be found at www.vianegativa.us/author/luisa

About Phoenicia Publishing

Phoenicia Publishing is an independent press based in Montreal but involved, through a network of online connections, with writers and artists all over the world. We are interested in words and images that illuminate culture, spirit, and the human experience. A particular focus is on writing and art about travel between cultures—whether literally, through lives of refugees, immigrants, and travelers, or more metaphorically and philosophically—with the goal of enlarging our understanding of one another through universal and particular experiences of change, displacement, disconnection, assimilation, sorrow, gratitude, longing and hope.

We are committed to the innovative use of the web and digital technology in all aspects of publishing and distribution, and to making high-quality works available that might not be viable for larger publishers. We work closely with our authors, and are pleased to be able to offer them a greater share of royalties than is normally possible.

Your support of this endeavor is greatly appreciated.

Our complete catalogue is online at www.phoeniciapublishing.com

CPSIA information can be obtained at www.ICGtesting.com
Printed in the USA
BVOW03s1529210914

367462BV00004B/17/P